MICROHABITATS

Life in a
HOUSE

Clare Oliver

Evans

Evans Brothers Limited

First published in Great Britain in 2002 by Evans Brothers Limited
2A Portman Mansions
Chiltern Street
London W1U 6NR

Project Editors: Sean Dolan, Tamsin Osler, Louise John
Consultant: Michael Chinery
Production Director: Richard Johnson
Illustrated by Stuart Lafford
Designed by Ian Winton

Planned and produced by Discovery Books

British Library Cataloguing in Publication Data
Oliver, Clare
    Life in a house - (Microhabitats)
    1. Household animals - Juvenile literature
    I. Title
    578.7'554

    ISBN 0 237 52303 5

Printed in the United States

Contents

In the House

Whose House?

Every house has an amazing variety of non-human lodgers – even yours! The warmth and shelter tempt minibeasts, birds and small mammals in from outside. Moths and craneflies fly in through open windows, attracted by electric lights.

Other creatures are born in the house and spend their whole life there. Holes in food packages are a telltale sign that insects or animals are raiding your food, but most creatures in the house feast on each other. You may never even notice that they are there.

Mildew

Spider

Silverfish

Bedbug

Dog flea

Other Life Forms

You may have house plants in your living room or potted herbs in your kitchen, but there are lots of other things growing in your home, too. **Fungus** grows on damp wallpaper. Furry green **mould** spreads across an old sandwich. And of course, billions of microscopic **bacteria** are multiplying all over the house. Fortunately, most are completely harmless to humans.

In the Kitchen

Creepy-Crawlies

The kitchen is a wonderful place for insects, especially cockroaches. However clean the room is, crumbs will linger on shelves or under cupboards. Cockroaches have midnight feasts on these leftovers. During the day, when people might tread on them, the insects slide their flat bodies into cracks in the walls and floor and hide.

Cockroaches will eat anything, from biscuits and pet food to cardboard and clothing.

Flour beetles will infest grain products such as flour and cereals.

Pest Prevention

Keep opened packages of sugar and flour in lidded containers. Flour is a favourite with flour mites and beetles. Wrap fresh food in plastic wrap or aluminum foil to keep insects out. Cheese and meat make the perfect 'nest' for a larder beetle, providing plenty of salty, protein-rich food for its **larvae**.

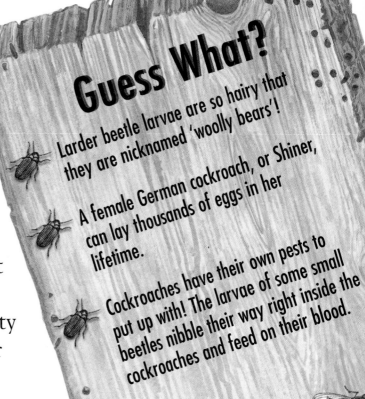

Guess What?

Larder beetle larvae are so hairy that they are nicknamed 'woolly bears'!

A female German cockroach, or Shiner, can lay thousands of eggs in her lifetime.

Cockroaches have their own pests to put up with! The larvae of some small beetles nibble their way right inside the cockroaches and feed on their blood.

7

Buzzing Around

Flies are always buzzing around the kitchen, especially during summer.

Housefly

Bluebottle

Some are houseflies, which have greyish bodies with yellowy speckles. But fruit flies and blowflies are common, too.

Greenbottle

Blowflies include bluebottles and greenbottles, both of which have shiny bodies.

Rotten Feasts

Flies eat food that has started to decay. Blowflies feed on rotten meat, including meaty pet food. Tiny fruit flies like soft, rotting fruit. Houseflies will feed on anything, including dung, which is why they can transmit so many diseases.

Baby Flies

Flies lay their eggs in or on food that can be eaten by their grubs when they hatch. A female housefly lays more than 100 eggs at a time. They take less than a day to hatch into maggots or larvae.

Maggots grow very quickly and, in warm conditions, can turn into adult flies within about 10 days.

Guess What?

The average housefly carries two million bacteria.

Houseflies' feet have tiny pads that cling to things. They allow them to scale a wall or walk upside-down on the ceiling!

Blowflies eat by vomiting saliva on to their food and then slurping it up. Sometimes they leave a bit just for you!

Furry Feeders

All over the world, house mice and brown rats live in people's homes, attracted by the warmth and free food. Mice do not **hibernate** if they live somewhere warm, and they are able to breed throughout the year.

Mice will eat cheese or, as this picture shows, pet food, but they prefer sugary foods, especially chocolate.

They live under the floorboards or behind kitchen cupboards. Sometimes they steal stuffing from a sofa or mattress to use as a cosy lining for their nest. They gnaw and squeeze through tiny holes in skirting boards or the backs of cupboards in search of food.

Rat Attack

Rats are larger than mice. They also visit the kitchen at night, using their keen sense of smell to sniff out food. Norway or brown rats (sometimes called sewer rats), pictured here, are most likely to live in the basement of a house. They are excellent swimmers and burrowers. Black rats are sometimes called ship rats. They are very rare in Britain but are most likely to be found near water and ports. All rats have extremely strong front teeth so that they can gnaw through all kinds of building materials.

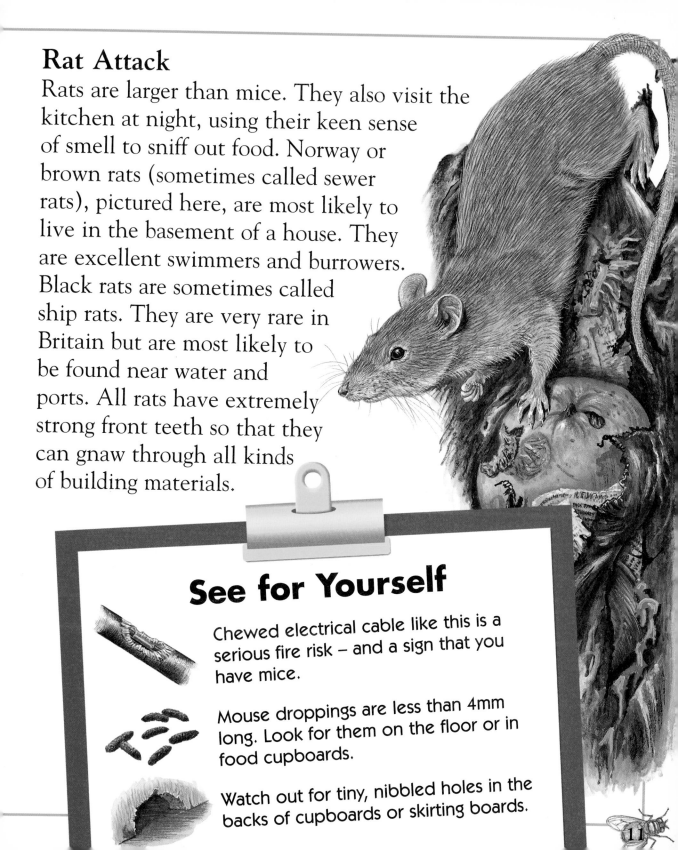

See for Yourself

Chewed electrical cable like this is a serious fire risk – and a sign that you have mice.

Mouse droppings are less than 4mm long. Look for them on the floor or in food cupboards.

Watch out for tiny, nibbled holes in the backs of cupboards or skirting boards.

Strange Diets

Household Hunters

All kinds of spiders live in your house, which is a very good thing. These useful **predators**

Long-legged cellar spider

keep insect pests under control. Common house spiders spin messy webs in dark corners. When an insect is caught in the web, the spider wraps the **prey** in silk and then bites it, injecting poison into it with its fangs. Sometimes spiders do not eat their prey right away, and you can find little food parcels hanging in webs round the house.

Many spiders chase their prey instead of catching them in a web. Zebra spiders live on outside walls and leap on to small flies. The woodlouse killer uses its huge jaws to catch woodlice.

This house spider has caught a fly in its web.

Scuttling Centipedes

The house centipede, which usually lurks under the floor, also eats household insects. It is about 5cm long and has 15 pairs of long, spindly legs. Once it has caught its insect prey, the centipede wrestles it to the ground and eats it.

The scariest thing about the house centipede is its speed – it can move 40cm in one second!

See for Yourself

This untidy web belongs to a house spider.

Likely to be found near a window or door, an orb web like this one was probably built by a garden spider.

Wood Munchers

Termites and carpenter ants like to munch on wood. In some parts of the world, especially the tropics, they are a big problem. When these insects get their strong teeth into the wood frame of a house, they can cause a lot of destruction.

Carpenter ants hollow out wood for their nests, and then come out at night to search for food, such as honeydew, fruit and meat. Termites also chew tunnels through the wood to make their nests, but they feed on the wood at the same time. They are able to digest **cellulose**, the tough tissue that is in wood.

Termites are related to wood roaches, which also eat cellulose. They digest it by keeping tiny animals called protozoa in their gut.

Termites make a tasty meal ou the bark and wood of a tree.

Every so often a wood roach eats its own droppings to make sure that it still has enough protozoa inside it to digest the wood.

Boring Beetles

Woodworms are beetle larvae that can reduce floorboards and window frames to dust. They can even munch their way through furniture! There are many different types of beetles, including furniture beetles and deathwatch beetles.

Life Cycle of a Woodworm

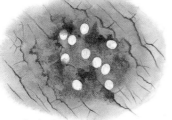

1. The adult beetle lays its eggs in cracks on the surface of the wood.

2. When the larva (grub) has hatched, it burrows through the wood, eating as it goes.

3. It may tunnel for as long as five years, then it turns into a pupa near the surface of the wood.

4. The new adult beetle pushes its way out of the wood. As it emerges, it chews an exit hole.

Book Lovers

Like wood, paper contains cellulose and makes a tasty, starchy feast for certain insects, such as booklice, roaches and termites. The paper is especially attractive when it is damp.

This booklouse has been magnified – in reality it is the size of the head of a pin.

Louse in the House

Most booklice have pale, soft bodies and are wingless. Although tiny, these insects have been known to destroy whole libraries. Booklice have long antennae (feelers) and a flat body that slips easily between the pages. Their pointy jaws cut through the paper which, as it passes through the insect's body, is turned into a fine powdery dust.

Fish Out of Water

Another bookshelf pest is the silverfish, an insect that has silvery scales and darts about very quickly. It prefers the dried-out, gluey binding of books.

Silverfish like damp places and are often found in kitchens and bathrooms, too.

Guess What?

Head lice are distant relatives of booklice. The jaws of a head louse are designed for sucking blood instead of chewing paper.

There are over 1,000 different types of booklice.

Silverfish don't only eat the bindings of books. They will also make a feast of flour, damp fabric, or even wallpaper paste!

Soft-bodied Bugs

Under Foot

Carpets and rugs are home to carpet beetles.
The adult beetle lays her eggs there so the
newly-hatched grubs can feast on fibres.

The grubs of the carpet beetle also like to eat fur and clothing.

The larvae make the floor a good hunting ground
for the kissing bug, a fierce masked hunter.
This is one of more than 4,000 species of assassin
bug. Its 'mask' or disguise is made of stuck-on bits
of carpet fluff and dust. Dust mites and carpet mites
also make their homes in carpets.

This picture shows what a dog flea looks like under a microscope.

Fleas

Houses with pet cats and dogs usually harbour fleas. Flea eggs fall off a pet's fur onto bedding or the carpet. After about 10 days, the tiny white eggs hatch into worm-like grubs. When the grubs grow into fleas, they can sense when an animal is approaching and spring into the air to hitch a ride in the animal's fur.

Guess What?

Fleas are the champion high-jumpers of the insect world in relation to their size. A cat flea can leap up to 34cm into the air.

Cat fleas will also bite humans, but some fleas are more picky. Penguin fleas only drink penguin blood!

Before we had houses full of carpets and other fabrics, carpet beetles and clothes moths used to live in birds' nests.

In the Bedroom

Seen through a magnifying glass, your mattress is covered with dust and storage mites that feed on flakes of skin. If you're unlucky there may also be bedbugs feeding on you, but these are big enough to see. Like all bugs, bedbugs have jaws that pierce the skin and are designed for sucking up liquid, especially your blood! Other bloodsuckers that sometimes cause problems are head and body lice that crawl in the hair and on the skin.

A magnified dust mite feeding on flakes of skin.

Wardrobe Pests

Not even your clothes are safe from insect pests. Clothes moth larvae can chew holes in your clothes. They like natural fibres such as wool or fur, but they also munch through synthetic fabrics.

Fabric is especially tasty to the clothes moth if it has traces of grease or sweat on it.

Lots of other insects like to eat away at your favourite clothes. Museum beetles eat all sorts of materials, while larder beetle larvae like leather. However, now that houses are warmer and drier, these pests are all less common.

Attics and Lofts

Owls and Bats

A house with an attic or loft space under the roof may have some unexpected lodgers staying there, taking advantage of its shelter, warmth, or food supply of mice, rats and insects. Bats and owls may also rest here during the day, as long as there's a hole for them to come in or out of. And despite their creepy reputation, bats really prefer warm, modern houses to dusty old ones!

This barn owl is leaving its roost for a night's hunting.

Night Hunters

Owls and bats both hunt under cover of darkness. Owls have such good hearing that they can pick up the quietest rustle made by a tiny animal in the undergrowth. Owls also rely on their sight when they hunt.

Little brown bats like these sometimes roost in the roof of a house.

Although folklore has it that bats are blind, most actually have good daytime vision. At night, however, they use a system called echolocation to help them hunt. By listening to the echoes made by their own high-pitched squeaks when they bounce off objects, bats can tell what is around them, including the insects they feed on.

Guess What?

Owls gulp down their prey whole, then spit up all the fur and bones later as a neat pellet.

In Europe edible and garden doormice often set up home in attics and make a lot of noise at night.

You may associate bats with vampires and Halloween spookiness, but in Asia bats are symbols of good luck.

Stinging Swarms

On summer days, you will often see wasps going in and out of the roof of a house.

Wasps are useful hunters of insects, but their sting is also painful – sometimes even deadly – to humans. This makes them annoying and even dangerous to have as visitors to or around your house.

Paper Sculpture

A paper wasp's nest looks like a work of art. The queen starts the nest by herself. When she has raised her first small brood of worker wasps, they take over the work of building the nest and feeding the grubs so she can lay eggs.

Guess What?

You can sometimes hear the scratching noise a wasp makes as it collects wood fibres for making a nest.

People who have an **allergic** reaction to a wasp sting can die without immediate medical treatment.

Only queens and worker wasps have a stinger. Most often, the stinger is used to defend the colony.

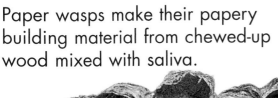

Paper wasps make their papery building material from chewed-up wood mixed with saliva.

Feathered Friends

Eaves protect the walls of a house from rain water. This makes them a good spot for small birds to nest. Tiny swallows and martins use sticky saliva to glue their mud and grass nests here, while swifts build nests of twigs, moss, or feathers. All of these birds are acrobatic fliers and as they swoop through the air, they keep their mouths open and snap up flying insects.

Swallow

This swallow is returning to her grass nest in the eaves of a house to feed her babies.

Chimney Nests

Because some birds choose chimney stacks as nesting sites, chimneys should be covered with fine-meshed wire. Such birds include chimney swifts, house sparrows and jackdaws.

This house swallow may make its nest in a chimney or a hollow, old tree.

See for Yourself

Look out for starlings nesting on your house. They make untidy nests of twigs and leaves, often wedged into gaps around drain pipes where they are sheltered by eaves.

This feather belongs to a barn owl. If you find one like this near your house, it could mean that a barn owl has made its nest in your attic.

Also watch for swallows around your house. They sometimes build their cup-shaped nests under the roofs of houses, usually on ledges or against a roof beam.

Your Home Under Threat

Pest Control

Whether they are big or small, animals that move into a house uninvited are usually unwelcome guests. Some, such as moths, are just a nuisance, but others can transmit disease and are dangerous. Ridding a house of pests is a job for experts. They are trained to use chemicals safely and will know exactly what to do.

This pest controller has special equipment and clothing.

What You Can Do

The best thing your family can do to prevent being overrun with pests is to keep the house clean.

Vacuuming the carpet reduces the population of dust mites, carpet beetles, and silverfish that live there.

Guess What?

Houses can be made termite-proof with concrete or treated-wood foundations.

Slugs reduce mildew on your bathroom tiles, but they leave behind a slimy trail of their own!

Towser, a cat that lived in Scotland, killed almost 29,000 mice in 24 years.

Storing food carefully leaves little to tempt mice, rats, or roaches into your kitchen. Above all, remember that every **microhabitat** is delicately balanced. Wiping out one important predator in a house could lead to a plague of its prey.

Glossary

Allergic: To have a sensitivity or severe reaction to foreign substances in the body.

Bacteria: Microscopic living things that are made up of a single cell and that split in two to reproduce themselves very quickly. Many bacteria cause diseases, such as cholera and many types of food poisoning.

Cellulose: The basic structural matter of plant cells.

Fungi: Plantlike organisms that include moulds, yeast, mildew and mushrooms.

Hibernation: Sleep-like state in which some animals survive winter.

Larva(e): An insect baby, such as a beetle grub, that is structurally different from its adult form.

Mammals: Warm-blooded animals, such as mice and bats, that give birth to live young and feed them on mother's milk.

Microhabitat: A small, specialised place, such as a house or flowerbed, where particular animals live and plants grow.

Mould: A type of fungus that is often found on old food, where it forms masses of tiny, woolly strands that are usually white, black, or greenish-grey.

Predators: Animals that hunt other animals for food.

Prey: Animals that are hunted by other animals for food.

Acknowledgements

The publishers would like to thank the following for permission to reproduce their pictures:
Front cover: Gerard Lacz/Frank Lane Picture Agency; p.6: Stephen Dalton/Natural History Photographic Agency; p.7: Stephen Dalton/Natural History Photographic Agency; p.9: Avril Ramage/Oxford Scientific Films; p.10: Jane Burton/Bruce Coleman Collection; p.12: London Scientific Films/Oxford Scientific Films; p.13: Raymond A.Mendez/Oxford Scientific Films; p.14: Kim Taylor/Bruce Coleman Collection; p.16: Kim Taylor/Bruce Coleman Collection; p.17: Stephen Dalton/Natural History Photographic Agency; p.18: John Downer/Oxford Scientific Films; p.19: Peter Parks/Oxford Scientific Films; p.20: David Scharf/Science Photo Library; p.21: John Downer/Oxford Scientific Films; p.22: Michael Callan/Frank Lane Picture Agency; p.23: Joe McDonald/Bruce Coleman Collection; p.25: John Mitchell/Oxford Scientific Films; p.26: R.Austing/Frank Lane Picture Agency; p.27: Chris Gomersall/Bruce Coleman Collection; p.28: Rentokil; p.29: Kath Walker.

Index